THEN & N

GAITHERSBURG

Shaun Curtis

To Rebecca, for all her love and support.

Copyright © 2010 by Shaun Curtis
ISBN 978-0-7385-8551-2

Library of Congress Control Number: 2009936602

Published by Arcadia Publishing
Charleston SC, Chicago IL, Portsmouth NH, San Francisco CA

Printed in the United States of America

For all general information contact Arcadia Publishing at:
Telephone 843-853-2070
Fax 843-853-0044
E-mail sales@arcadiapublishing.com
For customer service and orders:
Toll-Free 1-888-313-2665

Visit us on the Internet at www.arcadiapublishing.com

ON THE FRONT COVER: Frederick Avenue had been an ancient Native American trail long before George Washington passed by this location on his way to Frederick-Town. These photographs essentially mark the spot where Gaithersburg began in 1802, when Benjamin Gaither set up shop along the Great Road, as it was known then. It was a strategic location and was convenient for travelers to and from the Darnestown-Travilah and Barnesville areas. As Gaithersburg grew, so did Frederick Avenue. It remained largely residential until 1977, when the Maryland State Highway Administration began planning the widening of Frederick Avenue. The road was eventually widened from a two-lane country road to a six-lane divided highway. Most of the 19th-century structures were demolished, all of the street trees were removed, and many of the early-20th-century homes were sold and ultimately developed into shopping centers. Today Frederick Avenue is a bustling business corridor. (Then, courtesy of the City of Gaithersburg; now, courtesy of the author.)

ON THE BACK COVER: In 1893, Dr. Elisha C. Etchison purchased the corner property at Diamond and Summit Avenues from John B. Diamond and opened a drugstore. In addition to medicines, the store sold toiletries, novelties, and ice cream sodas that only cost a dime. Dr. W. D. Barnett later purchased the store. He is the man standing next to the telephone pole in this photograph, taken in 1920. In 1938, Dr. Barnett donated his extensive book collection and two rooms upstairs to the Homemakers' Club. Although the business at this site has changed owners several times over the years, there has always been a drugstore at this location. (Courtesy of the City of Gaithersburg.)

THEN & NOW

GAITHERSBURG

OPPOSITE: This photograph of downtown Gaithersburg was taken from the top of Bowman Mill in the mid-1950s. (Courtesy of the Gaithersburg Fire Museum.)

Contents

ACKNOWLEDGMENTS

I wish to thank the following people for their help: Frances Wilmot Kellerman, Michael Dwyer, Trudy Schwarz, Britta Monaco, Tom Nugent, Barbara Ramsdell Jones, Judy Christensen, George Winkler, Nancy Correll, Mary Margaret Garrett, Jim Davis, Garry Walker, Eva Foster, Keith Eig, Anne Kingsley, Gary Gloyd, and the folks at the Gaithersburg Community Museum. I would also like to extend a hand of gratitude to the authors of *Gaithersburg: The Heart of Montgomery County* (1978). Without this valuable reference, my book would not have been feasible.

Unless otherwise noted, all modern photographs are courtesy of the author.

INTRODUCTION

The community that became Gaithersburg actually started in the mid-1750s as a small gathering of a handful of families along an old Native American trail that is now Frederick Avenue. The settlement was known as Log Town and was located approximately where the pond at Summit Hall is today. Names such as Fulks, Burgess, DeSellum, Brookes, Gloyd, Diamond, and Gaither were some of the earliest families to settle in the area. The founding of Frederick-Town in 1745 and George Town in 1751 brought many travelers, who passed by Log Town on their way to and from these cities. By 1802, a man named Benjamin Gaither had become a leading figure, and he decided to set up a shop near present-day Frederick and Diamond Avenues. It was here, under the famous Forest Oak Tree that Gaither built his house. In a short time, blacksmiths, wheelwrights, and other tradesmen began to settle around Gaither's place. His establishment became known as Gaithersburg.

By the mid-19th century, Gaithersburg was a depressed area. The Chesapeake and Ohio (C&O) Canal was miles away, and the proposed railroad route was far from the city. Finally, in 1873, with the help of Francis Cassatt Clopper, the Metropolitan Branch of the Baltimore and Ohio (B&O) Railroad came to Gaithersburg. This was the single most important development in the history of the city.

The National Bureau of Standards moved its headquarters to Gaithersburg in 1961. A few years later, IBM and the National Geographic Society broke ground on new offices in the city. This brought an incredible amount of growth to Gaithersburg but also marked the end of an era. Gone were the days of farming and country living. Gone were the rolling fields of wheat. Agriculture was no longer the way of life for people in the city. Gaithersburg was becoming a fast-paced suburb of Washington, D.C.

For me, growing up in Gaithersburg during the 1980s and early 1990s was an adventure. There were still several undeveloped farms in the city for a kid to explore, including the Kentlands, as well as plenty of abandoned farmhouses in the woods. Much of Gaithersburg's past was fading away, but if you looked close enough, pieces of it were still around. Pretty soon, construction sites started popping up everywhere, and most of the land eventually became developed. While the city of Gaithersburg is a far different place than it was in the past, the rich history of this town and its people still shines bright today. I hope you enjoy reading my book as much as I enjoyed putting it together.

CHAPTER

1

EARLY SETTLEMENT

This is a glimpse at the remnants of Log Town at Summit Hall around 1885. Log Town was likely named after the prosperous lumber industry in the area. Baltus Fulks, who purchased the first two lots on this property, was among the earliest known inhabitants of what is now Gaithersburg. Original lots consisted of small log houses, vegetable gardens, and orchards. (Courtesy of the City of Gaithersburg.)

The Summit Hall property was later sold to James DeSellum, a prosperous farmer, who constructed a four-room log dwelling. During the Civil War, Gen. Jubal Early's Confederate troops were unwelcome guests at the DeSellum home. They took horses, livestock, and meat but missed the $3,000 that was hidden under Sarah DeSellum's skirt. The property was sold to Ignatius T. Fulks in 1886, who modernized the house, as shown in the photograph below. In 1936, the farm was sold to Frank Wilmot, who remodeled the house to its present state. (Then, courtesy of Frances Kellerman.)

The Summit Hall smokehouse, located behind the main house, is the oldest complete historic structure in Gaithersburg. At left, this photograph of Zoe Wilmot (left), Frances Wilmot Kellerman (center), and Lloyd Miller (right) was taken in 1936, when the Wilmots converted Summit Hall into the country's first commercial turf farm. Grass grown at Summit Hall can be found on the lawns of the White House, at the Washington Monument, and at Arlington National Cemetery. Today Summit Hall serves as a city recreational park. (Then, courtesy of Frances Kellerman.)

In 1844, Samuel Gloyd purchased the property on which the ancient Forest Oak Tree stood. This was also where Benjamin Gaither, for whom the city is named, originally built his house around 1802. Gloyd constructed his large Victorian home onto Gaither's original two-story log structure around 1844. By the late 1950s, increasing commercial development had made the property less valuable as a residence, and in 1957, the land was sold to the telephone company, and the house was demolished. Pictured above in 1950 is Todd Gloyd under the Forest Oak Tree. (Then, courtesy of the City of Gaithersburg.)

The famous Forest Oak Tree was close to 300 years old before a storm took it down in 1997. At one point, Gaithersburg was known as Forest Oak because of this massive landmark. Famous men such as George Washington and Edward Braddock passed under the Forest Oak during their travels between Georgetown and Frederick. Several large pieces of the tree were salvaged by the City of Gaithersburg to make commemorative plaques. (Now, courtesy of the City of Gaithersburg; then, courtesy of the Montgomery County Historical Society.)

A handful of mills existed along Seneca Creek as early as the Revolutionary War period. Francis Cassatt Clopper bought this gristmill from Zachariah Maccubbin in 1810. Clopper also operated a woolen factory nearby. In 1865, George Atzerodt, one of the conspirators involved in the assassination of Pres. Abraham Lincoln, spent a night here during his escape into Montgomery County. He was later caught up the road in Germantown. The mill was destroyed by fire in 1947. (Then, courtesy of Barbara Ramsdell Jones.)

Before the 1960s, the south end of Gaithersburg was known as Mount Pleasant, named by Col. Zadok Magruder, the first to settle in this area. In 1807, Magruder's son, Robert Pottinger Magruder, built this brick house near the intersection of Shady Grove Road and Frederick Avenue. By the early 1960s, the house was in ruins, and it was eventually demolished. Today the site where this house once stood is the parking lot of a Burger King. (Then, courtesy of Historic American Buildings Survey/ Library of Congress [HABS/LOC]; now, courtesy of E. Russell Gloyd.)

Another prominent figure in Gaithersburg's early history was Henry Brookes, who owned more than 1,000 acres in the northern part of what is now Gaithersburg. His home, Montpelier, was located at the intersection of Frederick and Montgomery Village Avenues. The house stood on this site for close to 175 years until IBM constructed offices here in 1966. The house was demolished to make way for IBM's parking lot. (Then, courtesy of the George Beall Collection/Maryland–National Capital Park and Planning Commission [M-NCPPC].)

The Diamonds were among the social and business leaders of Gaithersburg. John Bernard Diamond helped start the Gaithersburg Milling and Manufacturing Company in 1891. In 1892, he purchased this property and built his home, called Zoar, which was located on Quince Orchard Road. Zoar was demolished in 1973 to make way for the Watkins-Johnson Company building. (Then, courtesy of the George Beall Collection/ M-NCPPC.)

The Fulks family has been a part of Gaithersburg's history since the 1760s. Thomas Fulks was a prominent businessman, farmer, and Gaithersburg politician. His house, located at 208 South Frederick Avenue, is a well-preserved example of late-19th-century architecture and has undergone little exterior alteration since the beginning of the 20th century. The photograph below was taken in 1897, the same year the house was built. (Then, courtesy of the City of Gaithersburg.)

AGRICULTURE

This was one of the many prosperous farms that reflected Gaithersburg's status as an agricultural powerhouse during the late 19th and early 20th centuries. Originally owned by the Briggs family, this farm was located right off old Quince Orchard Road. It was later owned by William Johnston. By 1974, when this photograph was taken, the farm was in decline. Today this land is part of the Quince Orchard Park neighborhood. (Courtesy of Michael Dwyer/M-NCPPC.)

In addition to machinery and fertilizer, farmers also needed good-quality work animals. Local farmers could buy or sell horses and mules at William Dosh's stable, located near the corner of Brookes and Summit Avenues. In the late 1950s, Dosh was forced to close his business after the town council passed an ordinance forbidding livestock in downtown Gaithersburg. He sold his stable, consisting of 40 stalls, and apartment buildings were constructed on this site. (Then, courtesy of the City of Gaithersburg.)

In 1917, Thomas and Company constructed the Thomas Cannery in Gaithersburg. At first, the factory canned corn and pumpkin, but it quickly switched to corn and peas because pumpkin produced too much waste. During the summer months, canning went on all day and night as crops were harvested on local farms. The Thomas Cannery closed in 1962, and in 2004, the building was restored for commercial use. (Then, courtesy of the City of Gaithersburg.)

In 1938, local businessman Eugene B. Casey built his dairy barn at the south end of Gaithersburg. The 60 cows at the dairy barn produced 300 gallons of milk a day, which was sold to local dairies. Casey's barn soon became a local landmark when it was used as a signboard for political candidates in the 1940s. In 1971, when the photograph below was taken, Casey deeded the barn and land to the City of Gaithersburg for use as a community center. (Then, courtesy of the City of Gaithersburg.)

Before 1850, the Montgomery County Fair was held in Rockville, where Richard Montgomery High School is now located. When the fair outgrew that land, the Gaithersburg site was selected because of its good roads and proximity to the railroad. Close to 1,000 volunteers gathered on June 4, 1949, to construct most of the livestock exhibits, and the first fair was held that same year. In 2008, the Montgomery County Fair experienced record attendance—225,000 visitors. (Then, courtesy of the City of Gaithersburg.)

Crown Farm is a 180-acre farm that includes two 19th-century houses, several agricultural buildings, and a log house that dates back to the early 1800s. The farm is located on Fields Road, across the street from the Washingtonian Center, and is one of the only remaining pieces of original farmland in the area. Crown Farm was slated for development in 2009, but developers backed out once the economy soured. (Then, courtesy of Michael Dwyer/M-NCPPC.)

Southern States Co-op opened in the 1930s to serve farmers and the agricultural community at large, selling feed, seed, fertilizer, and farm supplies. The company, based in Richmond, Virginia, offered a much wider variety of products than locally owned businesses. Goods shipped from Richmond to Washington, D.C., were easily transported via railroad to the Gaithersburg store location, which was strategically located near the train station along Summit Avenue. (Then, courtesy of the City of Gaithersburg.)

In the 1920s, the Bowman brothers of Germantown built a mill on Diamond Avenue that was in operation until the 1960s. This mill was an important early-20th-century link between Gaithersburg's agricultural community and the railroad. Today the mill has been preserved into Granary Row, complete with small shops, a restaurant, and an automotive service center. (Then, courtesy of the City of Gaithersburg.)

CHAPTER 3

THE RAILROAD AND COMMERCIAL DEVELOPMENT

Gaithersburg's growth and prosperity can be attributed to the coming of the railroad. The completion of the Metropolitan Branch of the Baltimore and Ohio (B&O) Railroad in 1873 created an incredible amount of commercial activity and was the single most important development in the city's history. (Courtesy of the City of Gaithersburg.)

The present train station was built in 1884 on the east side of Summit Avenue. It originally had two separate waiting rooms, one for men and the other for women. In 1978, the B&O Railroad Station was listed on the National Register of Historic Places, the first historic site in the city to receive such an honor. Today the restored station continues to serve as a ticket station, with daily service to Washington, D.C., and to many cities in Maryland. The station also serves as a coffee shop and as a place for locomotive enthusiasts to watch the trains pass by. (Then, courtesy of the City of Gaithersburg.)

THE RAILROAD AND COMMERCIAL DEVELOPMENT

The old freight house is located next to the train station and has been restored to its original condition. The Gaithersburg Community Museum now occupies the freight house and features educational exhibits, historical photographs, and a large model railroad display. Outside, the rolling stock exhibit features historic trains that people can explore. (Then, courtesy of the Gaithersburg Community Museum.)

The railroad would never have come to Gaithersburg, or to most of Montgomery County, if not for the efforts of Francis Cassatt Clopper. Clopper and generations of his family lived at the Woodlands Estate until 1953, when the State of Maryland bought the property. The house later burned down. There is a great deal of history associated with this site. Today a short, self-guided trail interprets the life and the estate of the Clopper family. This tour is located where the house once stood, near the visitors' center at Seneca Creek State Park. (Then, courtesy of HABS/LOC.)

THE RAILROAD AND COMMERCIAL DEVELOPMENT

Not far from the Woodlands Estate, down Game Preserve Road, is a stone tunnel built around 1906. It was near this tunnel that the B&O Railroad built Clopper his own station. The undated photograph at left shows an unidentified member of the Clopper family under the newly constructed railroad underpass. Clopper's Station is no longer standing, but the original tunnel is still there. (Then, courtesy of Barbara Ramsdell Jones.)

In 1873, the commercial center of Gaithersburg began to shift from Frederick Avenue to the area around Diamond and Summit Avenues to be closer to the railroad station. Soon merchants, farmers, and businessmen started opening up shops around the area known as Olde Towne today. The early- 20th-century photograph above of Diamond Avenue as a dirt road shows the side of Gartner's Funeral Home and Furniture Store, the second building on the right, and the Belt Building on the left. (Then, courtesy of the City of Gaithersburg.)

THE RAILROAD AND COMMERCIAL DEVELOPMENT

This location has been a drugstore since Elisha C. Etchison purchased the property from John B. Diamond in 1893. The drugstore remained in the Etchison family for several years before becoming Barnett's, Lynn's, and eventually Diamond Drug.

The photograph below, taken in 1920, shows the store when a Dr. Barnett owned it. Barnett is the man standing next to the telephone pole. (Then, courtesy of the City of Gaithersburg.)

By the late 1890s, trains stopped several times a day in Gaithersburg. Now that there was a bustling commercial district in town, traveling salesmen needed a place to stay. John Diamond and Ignatius Fulks opened the Forest Oak Hotel along Diamond Avenue. As the trains arrived, hotel manager Richard Miles would send his porters to the railroad to advertise the rates and conveniences of the Forest Oak Hotel. (Then, courtesy of the City of Gaithersburg.)

THE RAILROAD AND COMMERCIAL DEVELOPMENT

Next door to the hotel was Richard Murphy's house and tinsmith shop. This was an era when tin roofs and spouting were more commonplace than today. Murphy was listed as Gaithersburg's only tinsmith in the 1900 census. His place was located approximately where McCormick Paints is today. (Then, courtesy of the City of Gaithersburg.)

The First National Bank of Gaithersburg opened in 1891 on the corner of Diamond and Summit Avenues. During the Great Depression, the bank brought a sense a security to the town by continuing business as usual with its customers. In 1960, the bank merged with Suburban Trust. Although the bank has lost its original steepled roofline, many parts of the building have not changed in more than 100 years. (Then, courtesy of the City of Gaithersburg.)

THE RAILROAD AND COMMERCIAL DEVELOPMENT

The Gaithersburg Milling and Manufacturing Company was founded in 1891 by local businessmen and farmers, with Ignatius T. Fulks serving as president and major stockholder. The steam-powered mill was built parallel to the train tracks along Diamond Avenue and manufactured feeds, fertilizers, and flour. The plant grew to be one of the wealthiest operations in Montgomery County. The mill eventually burned down in 1910. (Then, courtesy of the City of Gaithersburg.)

The photograph below, taken around 1920, shows Summit Avenue looking toward the train station. John Nicholl's Harness and Horse Furnishing Business was one of the most successful industries in Gaithersburg during the early 20th century. Nicholls manufactured saddles and harnesses and sold carriages, buggies, whips, and sleigh bells. William J. Cooke and Charles F. Hogan each had a carriage-making factory in town as well. (Then, courtesy of the City of Gaithersburg.)

THE RAILROAD AND COMMERCIAL DEVELOPMENT

The Summit Hotel was regarded as a trendy spring and summer resort for those who wished to take a holiday from the fast-paced life of Washington, D.C. The hotel, seen above in 1895, was located at the corner of Summit and Frederick Avenues where Saint Martin's Church now stands. The elegant hotel could accommodate as many as 100 guests and was known for its pleasant atmosphere and good food. The hotel burned to the ground on January 5, 1904. (Then, courtesy of the City of Gaithersburg.)

Carson Ward, a prominent businessman and citizen, opened his general store in 1890 on the corner of Brookes and Frederick Avenues. He is the man standing on the right next to, from left to right, John Ward, Clarence Case, Laura Ward, and George Darby in 1919. Ward's building also served as town hall in 1912. Although this structure has been extensively rebuilt by its owner, Mattress Discounters, care was taken to preserve the appearance of the building. (Then, courtesy of the City of Gaithersburg.)

Carson Ward, who was mayor of Gaithersburg from 1904 to 1906, also owned one of the first gas stations in Gaithersburg. The station was located across Brookes Avenue from his original general store. This site remained a gas station for many years until the early 1980s, when Frederick Avenue was widened and the bridge over the railroad tracks was expanded. (Then, courtesy of the City of Gaithersburg.)

In the 1930s, Tommy Waters opened a drugstore and soda fountain business in the original Ward Store building. This was a popular place to relax and socialize, especially for teenagers. Anne Kingsley, who grew up in Gaithersburg, fondly remembers stopping in for a Coca-Cola at Waters Drug Store with her friends during her high school days. (Then, courtesy of the City of Gaithersburg.)

CHAPTER 4

COMMUNITY LIFE

There have been many community events, clubs, and social organizations in Gaithersburg's history, but none has lasted longer than the annual Labor Day Parade. Here is the Labor Day Parade in 1959 as it passes down Frederick Avenue. (Courtesy of the City of Gaithersburg.)

The Gaithersburg Labor Day Parade was started in 1938 by the Gaithersburg–Washington Grove Fire Department as a major fund-raising activity. Since then, the only year Gaithersburg did not have a parade was 1942, because of World War II. While the parade routes have changed over the years, the community still gathers each Labor Day to see the floats and fire engines. (Then, courtesy of E. Russell Gloyd.)

John A. Belt brought his business to town to take advantage of the railroad. By the beginning of the 20th century, his emporium was one of the largest in Montgomery County. Belt was also an active civic leader in Gaithersburg, and his building was the preferred location for lectures, theater, recitals, musical presentations, and high school graduations. Belt's first wood-frame building burned down and was rebuilt in the same place in 1903, when the photograph below was taken. (Then, courtesy of the City of Gaithersburg.)

The original Gaithersburg School was formerly located where Gaithersburg Elementary School now stands at 35 North Summit Avenue. Built in 1904, the school initially provided an elementary program for grades one to seven and a three-year high school program. By the late 1940s, the school was overcrowded, and was later demolished. Construction of the present-day Gaithersburg High School commenced at 314 South Frederick Avenue. The new school opened in 1951. (Now, courtesy of E. Russell Gloyd; then, courtesy of the City of Gaithersburg.)

The Meem family sits in front of Martha Meem's house in the above photograph, taken in the late 1800s. Martha Meem clearly intended for her property to be developed as a prestigious neighborhood with grand houses. In 1879, she built this French Second Empire–inspired house at 104 Chestnut Street. Meem owned 200 acres around Chestnut Street, and her land stayed in the family until 1934. (Then, courtesy of the City of Gaithersburg.)

The building that now houses Gaithersburg's city government offices and council chambers was originally a private residence built in 1895 by Rosa and Henry Miller. In 1913, this 5-acre estate was purchased by Edward P. Schwartz, a successful realtor from Washington, D.C. The Schwartz home was the first residence in Gaithersburg to have electricity. The house was purchased by the City of Gaithersburg in 1958 and turned into the Gaithersburg Civic Center, or city hall. (Then, courtesy of the City of Gaithersburg.)

Edward Schwartz, the man pictured below in the white shirt, was an avid gardener. Between 1914 and 1923, he imported peonies from all over the world so that, by 1923, he had more than 410 varieties growing in his garden. Every spring, people would come to see his beautiful display, including Pres. Woodrow Wilson. In 1946, the peonies were moved to a farm on Clopper Road, which was eventually incorporated into Seneca Creek State Park, where they continue to bloom today. (Now, courtesy of Patricia Lawrence; then, courtesy of the City of Gaithersburg.)

The Gaither Theater, previously named the Lyric Theater, was built by Paul and Hobart Ramsdell along Frederick Avenue between Diamond and Brookes Avenues. It was the only theater in town for many years. The building burned down in the mid-1990s, but by then, it was being used to sell ready-made kitchen cabinets. (Then, courtesy of the Montgomery County Historical Society.)

In 1898, the International Geodetic Association established a network of observatories to measure the wobble of the planet on its axis by plotting the locations of specific stars. The highest point of Summit Hall Farm in Gaithersburg was chosen, together with sites around the world. Knowledge gained from the observations helped assist scientists in the study of the Earth's geophysical makeup and aided spacecraft orbiting the planet. The observatory closed in 1982, when computers took over the job. (Then, courtesy of the City of Gaithersburg.)

Most of the shops along Diamond Avenue have always been, and still are, family owned and operated. In an age when chain stores dominate the majority of shopping districts, the absence of them along Diamond Avenue adds to the hometown atmosphere. (Then, courtesy of E. Russell Gloyd.)

King Pontiac was located at 312 East Diamond Avenue. It is shown here in 1960. W. Lawson King owned this business and a number of retail establishments in Old Towne, as well as many farms in Montgomery County. He was called "Mr. Gaithersburg" for both his business and personal interests in the town's welfare. King Pontiac later moved to the corner of Shady Grove Road and Frederick Avenue and is still in business today. (Then, courtesy of the City of Gaithersburg.)

Walter Byrne operated a meat market and small grocery store at 125 East Diamond Avenue. Local farmers often brought their sausage meat to him for grinding and traded their farm-fresh eggs and butter for merchandise. Later the McMurtray family owned and operated Gaithersburg Floral Arts in this building from 1967 until 2007. (Then, courtesy of Eva Foster.)

Built in 1926 on the grounds of Walter Magruder's 106-acre Rolling Acres dairy farm, Asbury Methodist Village was originally a Methodist home for the aged and orphaned. The community rapidly grew into a sophisticated yet caring place where seniors of all denominations could enjoy a productive and healthy retirement. High-rise apartment buildings now stand on land where milk cows once grazed. (Then, courtesy of the Library of Congress.)

The Bowman Mill illustrates the concept of endurance. The mill was twice destroyed by fire, in 1943 and again in 1987. When a local developer purchased the mill in 1993, it was noted that all the feed bins were still intact, as were the auger used for grinding feed and the grain distribution machine. The mill, renamed Granary Row, was the winner of the 1997 Merit Award by the Maryland Society of American Institute of Architects. Pictured above is the mill on fire on November 6, 1943. (Then, courtesy of the City of Gaithersburg.)

The brick fire station for the Gaithersburg–Washington Grove Fire Department was built at 13 East Diamond Avenue in 1930 to replace a two-stall metal building constructed nearby in 1895. The building included a six-lane bowling alley that was used to raise operating funds for the department. The station closed in 1977, when a new station on Montgomery Village Avenue was built. Today the old fire station is the Gaithersburg Fire Museum. (Then, courtesy of the Gaithersburg Fire Museum.)

The Kinsey family owned and operated a gas station at 408 North Frederick Avenue until the mid-1970s, when it was sold to its current owners, the Shipe family, who opened an Exxon station. The *c.* 1956 photograph below shows Kinsey's station shortly after it was remodeled. There was a coin-operated Laundromat on the property as well. The building behind Kinsey's later became Dalamar Bowling Lanes and Roller Rink and today is the Golden Bull Restaurant. (Then, courtesy of the Gaithersburg Exxon.)

In the 1950s, there was nothing across the street from Kinsey's. Most of this area along Frederick Avenue was residential back then. Safeway constructed a large store across the street in the early 1960s and stayed there for years. In the 1980s, there was an electronics store called Luskin's in this location. (Then, courtesy of the Gaithersburg Exxon.)

In 1947, Bill Norman opened the Gaithersburg Lumber and Supply Company along Route 355. In 1985, this entire site was demolished to make way for the Frederick Avenue Bridge over the railroad tracks. Gaithersburg Lumber moved to the other side of Route 355, just a few hundred yards away, and changed its name to Barron's Lumber. (Then, courtesy of the Jim Davis.)

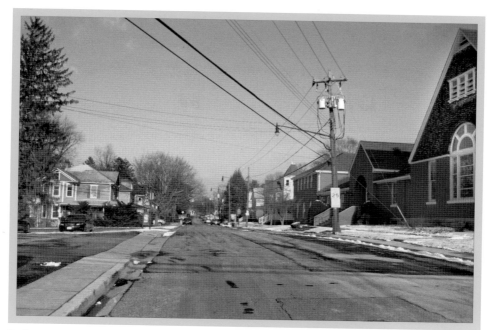

Walker Avenue is the most consistent street in Gaithersburg's historic district. Most of its houses were built between 1904 and 1930. The street is named after John Walker, whose farm became Walker Avenue when he decided to subdivide the front end of it in 1904. Many notable people have lived on Walker Avenue, including a few mayors of Gaithersburg, the Montgomery County chief of police, a member of the House of Delegates in Annapolis, and the principal of Gaithersburg's school. (Then, courtesy of the City of Gaithersburg.)

GAITHERSBURG MD.
Walker Avenue

Gaithersburg's original post office was established on August 4, 1851, and was called the Forest Oak Post Office. In those days, stagecoaches delivered mail to residents. When the first passenger trains began operating in 1873, the railroad system was given the town's mail contract. The location of the post office moved around a few times and, in 1960, ended up at its present location at 21 South Summit Avenue. (Then, courtesy of the City of Gaithersburg.)

COMMUNITY LIFE

Here is a great view of the Frederick and Brookes Avenues intersection in the 1950s. By this time, Bill Reber operated a novelty shop and soda fountain business in the original Ward Store building. The sign on the side of his store advertises "tourists needs, film, cigars smokers needs" and, of course, a soda fountain. Today this intersection is not a busy commercial district like it once was, but many of the original structures still exist. (Then, courtesy of E. Russell Gloyd.)

The Gaithersburg Ice House was located at 107 East Diamond Avenue. The building was originally constructed in 1913 for the Purity Ice Company. During the 1920s, the mayor of Gaithersburg, Williams McBain, and his son David started the Rockville and Gaithersburg Ice Company. Before the days of modern refrigeration, customers would place a large card in their windows indicating how much ice they wanted delivered. In 1977, the building became Keg City and sold beer. Today this building houses a Mexican restaurant and a check-cashing business. (Then, courtesy of the City of Gaithersburg.)

The Holiday Motel is another interesting building that has vanished. Constructed around 1945, the motel was located at 807 South Frederick Avenue. As a child, the author remembers driving by this building with his parents and thinking that it looked haunted. For a time, the Holiday Motel was the site of a cable television station, the source of the transmitter tower to the left of the house. It was also the site of the *Gaithersburg Gazette* offices for a number of years. Now in its place is an EZ Storage business. (Then, courtesy of Judy Christensen.)

Dede's Diner was located on Darnestown Road near the intersection of Route 28 and Quince Orchard Road. It was owned and operated by Dede McMahon, who bought the place in 1967. Some of the author's earliest memories are of early Saturday morning breakfasts at Dede's with his father. Dede made some amazing pancakes. The property was sold to the Potomac Garden Center in 1991, and the diner was demolished a few years later. (Then, courtesy of Dede McMahon.)

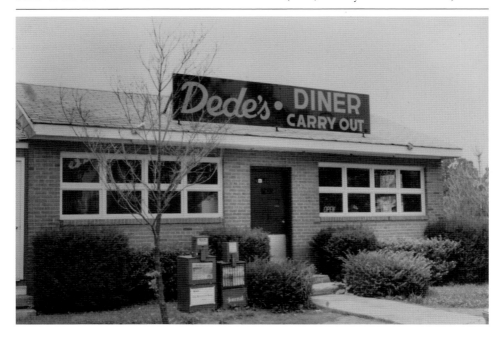

COMMUNITY LIFE

CHAPTER 5

GROWTH AND DEVELOPMENT

The first period of major growth for Gaithersburg occurred when the railroad came to the city in the 1870s. By the 1960s, Gaithersburg was entering its second period of rapid growth, largely due to the decentralization of federal government offices during this time. Many jobs were created in the area, and an influx of housing developments sprang up, like the West Riding and Diamond Farms neighborhoods, shown here in 1972. (Then, courtesy of E. Russell Gloyd.)

These pictures were taken near the southwest corner of North Frederick Avenue and what was then called Brown Station Road (now Montgomery Village Avenue). The photograph above was taken in 1964. The railroad overpass and the I-270 bridge can barely be seen in the distance. The barns on the right were part of the old Brookes property, which is now IBM. (Then, courtesy of Barbara and Albert Zanner Jr.)

On June 14, 1961, the National Bureau of Standards (now NIST) broke ground on its first building in Gaithersburg. Since that day, the population of the city has grown from 8,000 to more than 50,000 residents. The relocation of this government agency was the catalyst for the second period of major growth and development for the city. (Both, courtesy of the National Institute of Standards and Technology.)

Roseanne Gardens Apartments was built by Eugene Casey in 1966 at the intersection of Frederick Avenue and West Deer Park Road. During the 1950s and 1960s, the demand for apartment living in Gaithersburg was high. There was even a waiting list to get into many apartment buildings. Roseanne Gardens Apartments has recently been torn down to make way for approximately 315 apartment units with a parking garage, 28 condominiums, and 53 townhouse units. (Then, courtesy of the Montgomery County Historical Society.)

GROWTH AND DEVELOPMENT

Remus Dorsey, who was a Montgomery County commissioner, died in 1892. In his will, he left his sister, Annie E. Trundle, his house. The Trundle house was located on West Diamond Avenue where Barron's Lumber is today. It was one of the oldest buildings in the city. The overnight loss of this significant and historical landmark to development was the catalyst for the City of Gaithersburg's present historic preservation ordinance. (Then, courtesy of the City of Gaithersburg.)

In 1956, developer and builder Sam Eig constructed the Washingtonian Motel on what was then an isolated outpost along Interstate 70 (now I-270). The Washington Redskins stayed at the motel and practiced on the football field located on the property. The motel was expanded during the next 10 years but was badly damaged by fire in 1976. It was rebuilt but eventually closed 10 years later. Today the site is a Marriott Suites Hotel, and I-270 is much wider. (Then, courtesy of Keith Eig.)

In the mid-1960s, Sam Eig built the 26-story Washingtonian Towers Apartments, the nation's first luxury apartment building to be constructed at the center of a golf course. The surrounding area remained largely rural well into the 1980s. Today the golf course is the busy Washingtonian Center, where the old building sits among hotels, parking garages, and restaurants. (Then, courtesy of E. Russell Gloyd.)

Builder Sam Eig also owned the Shady Grove Music Fair, which was just a hundred yards from the Washingtonian Motel. Shady Grove was the venue of choice in the Washington area for movie stars, bands, plays, and musicals during the 1960s and 1970s. It was an arena theater where the audience surrounded the stage. Acts such as James Brown, Bruce Springsteen, Rod Stewart, and the Jackson 5 performed here. Many high school graduations were held here, as well. Today the site is office buildings. (Then, courtesy of E. Russell Gloyd.)

Echo Dale was the name of Douglas Clopper's farm. It was located on land that is now the Bennington neighborhood. Douglas Clopper was Francis Cassatt Clopper's son and was born at the Woodlands Estate, just up the road from Echo Dale. In the 1850s, Douglas Clopper built his house, which sat about where the separate group of trees are on the left in the aerial photograph below, which shows the construction of the Bennington neighborhood in 1972. (Then, courtesy of Barbara Ramsdell Jones; now, courtesy of Russell Gloyd.)

At one time, Frederick Avenue crossed directly over the train tracks at Diamond Avenue. Watchmen were employed to guard the crossing, but accidents continued to occur. In 1928, the death of popular parish priest Rev. John Stanislaus Cuddy roused the community to action, and they demanded the crossing be eliminated. Two years later, in 1930, the bridge over the railroad was complete. Fifty-five years later, in 1985, this bridge was demolished to make way for a new one. (Then, courtesy of the City of Gaithersburg.)

Diamond Square Shopping Center was built in 1977. Giant Food, Baskin-Robbins, a dry cleaner, and a restaurant called Shakey's were some of the first businesses built at Diamond Square. The shopping center's close proximity to the NIST campus made it a success from the start. Today Giant Food is the only original business left in the shopping center. (Then, courtesy of the Montgomery County Historical Society.)

Another old house that was lost to development was the Mills House, located on Muddy Branch Road near the I-270 bridge. The land on which this Colonial house sat belonged to Charles Saffell, father-in-law to Richard Henry Mills. Richard Mills and his family, pictured below, lived in this house for many years before it was demolished to make way for the Montgomery Club Apartments in 1985. (Both, courtesy of the Gaithersburg Community Museum.)

GROWTH AND DEVELOPMENT

With growth came the need for wider roads. Many small country roads in the city were expanded to handle the ever-increasing amount of traffic. In 1986, Muddy Branch Road was widened to four lanes. Notice on the right that the Washingtonian Woods neighborhood did not exist yet. This was then the site of the Washingtonian Golf Course, also owned by Sam Eig. (Then, courtesy of Tom Marchessault.)

Great Seneca Highway is 8 miles long and was built to connect Germantown, Gaithersburg, and Rockville. The first section, between Clopper and Middlebrook Roads, opened in 1987. The section between Route 28 and Quince Orchard Road opened in 1989, and the section between Quince Orchard and Clopper Roads opened in June 1990. The photograph above shows the construction of the highway at Muddy Branch Road, looking toward Germantown. (Then, courtesy of Tom Marchessault.)

Maple Spring Farm was located at the corner of Darnestown and Dufief Mill Roads. William Garrett's house was built around 1879 and is an example of typical vernacular architecture constructed in Montgomery County during the late 19th century. The house was significantly altered during construction of an attached brick medical center. The outbuildings include a large dairy barn, a hay barn, and two garages. The dairy barn was used as a veterinary clinic for years. (Then, courtesy of Mary Margaret Garrett.)

Lakeforest Mall opened in 1978. At the time it was the largest indoor retail mall in the county and featured four major department stores, a stage for the performing arts, and an ice-skating rink, which was later turned into a movie theater. The movie theater has since been converted into a food court. (Both, courtesy of the Montgomery County Historical Society.)

Opening ceremonies for Lakeforest Mall were held on September 12, 1978. The author remembers playing in this center area as a child and throwing coins into the fountain. While the mall has changed dramatically, it is still packed with families and shoppers every weekend, especially during the holidays. (Then, courtesy of the Montgomery County Historical Society.)

The Tschiffely-Kent property has been a local landmark for more than 100 years. The brick mansion was built in 1900 by Frederick A. Tschiffely Jr., who owned a wholesale drugstore business in Washington, D.C. In 1942, the 602-acre farm was sold to Otis Beall Kent, who dramatically changed the main house, outbuildings, and the surrounding property. Kent was a strong advocate for wildlife preservation and added ponds and lakes on his property to provide habitat for birds. (Then, courtesy of the City of Gaithersburg.)

GROWTH AND DEVELOPMENT

The barn was also built in 1900 by Frederick A. Tschiffely Jr. and was used as a stable for his horses. Shown here is Otis Kent in the early 1940s. Today the building is home to the Gaithersburg Arts Barn, where visitors can attend workshops and classes, observe artists at work in studios, and enjoy performances in the barn's 99-seat theater. (Then, courtesy of the City of Gaithersburg.)

Just a few hundred feet down a hill from the mansion is a large round garden lined with quartz rocks. This round stonework forms the top of an unused crypt or grotto that was built by Frederick A. Tschiffely Jr. around 1900. In the 1990s, a house was constructed next to the grotto, and the owner filled the structure in with dirt to prevent animals from making it their home. (Then, courtesy of the City of Gaithersburg.)

GROWTH AND DEVELOPMENT

According to R. Humphrey Cissel, grandson of Frederick Tschiffely Jr., this springhouse was on the property before the family purchased the land in the 1853. All that is left is the foundation, but the spring is still active, which can be clearly seen upon visiting the site. The springhouse remains can be found on the edge of Inspiration Lake in the Kentlands community. (Then, courtesy of the City of Gaithersburg.)

Above is an early photograph of the Tschiffely Gatehouse, the home of Jim Wood (pictured), the family cook, and his dog. The gatehouse was located at the Darnestown Road entrance of the farm. In the 1940s, Kent dramatically changed the gatehouse from its original architecture. The building was eventually demolished, and a replica of the house was constructed and put up for sale in 1989. (Then, courtesy of the City of Gaithersburg.)

GROWTH AND DEVELOPMENT

During the early 20th century, Frederick Tschiffely Jr. allowed Montgomery County to operate a quarry on his property. This small quarry provided the rocks to build many of the local roads back then. The quarry was located off of what is now Little Quarry Road in the Kentlands neighborhood. (Then, courtesy of the City of Gaithersburg.)

The amount of development Gaithersburg has experienced from 1957 to 2006 is illustrated in these aerial photographs. One can clearly see the shift from an agricultural community to a busy suburban city. The I-270 interchange is at the top right-hand side of the photographs. Notice there was no lake at Seneca Creek State Park in 1957. Clopper Lake was dug out and flooded in 1975. One wonders what the people who owned these farms 100 years ago would think of their land today. (Both, courtesy of the USDA.)

GROWTH AND DEVELOPMENT

Longdraft Estates were built in 1984 on a dairy farm originally owned by W. O. Dosh. According to legend, Dosh won the farm in a poker game by getting his opponent intoxicated and sitting him in front of a large mirror, where he could see his cards. Where the tree-line ends on the right-hand side of both pictures (taken in 1974 and 1984, respectively) is today the intersection of Quince Orchard Road and Great Seneca Highway. (Then, courtesy of Michael Dwyer/M-NCPPC; now, courtesy of Michael Blongiewicz.)

While most of the surrounding old farms and houses in Gaithersburg have been developed with little or no trace of the past left behind, the original downtown Gaithersburg has been, for the most part, well preserved. Olde Towne is the site of the city's original mercantile district, and important historic structures like the Belt building, the Bank building, and the train station are still standing and looking better than ever. (Then, courtesy of the Gaithersburg Fire Museum.)

GROWTH AND DEVELOPMENT

Shaun Curtis was born and raised in Gaithersburg. As a child, he spent countless hours exploring the remains of what Gaithersburg once was. Witnessing 20 years of development spurred a desire to document the remaining historic places throughout town. What started as a weekend pastime has resulted in the production of this book. The photographs shown here are of the author at Crown Farm in 2009.

www.arcadiapublishing.com

Discover books about the town where you grew up, the cities where your friends and families live, the town where your parents met, or even that retirement spot you've been dreaming about. Our Web site provides history lovers with exclusive deals, advanced notification about new titles, e-mail alerts of author events, and much more.

Arcadia Publishing, the leading local history publisher in the United States, is committed to making history accessible and meaningful through publishing books that celebrate and preserve the heritage of America's people and places. Consistent with our mission to preserve history on a local level, this book was printed in South Carolina on American-made paper and manufactured entirely in the United States.

Find Your Place in History.